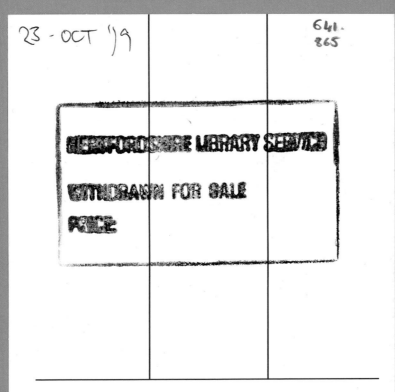
Please renew or return items by the date shown on your receipt

www.hertfordshire.gov.uk/libraries

Renewals and enquiries: 0300 123 4049

Textphone for hearing or 0300 123 4041
speech impaired users:

L32 11.16

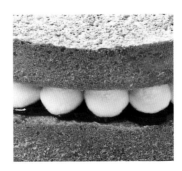

the PINK WHISK
guide to
CAKE MAKING

the PINK WHISK guide to CAKE MAKING

D&C
David and Charles

CONTENTS

INTRODUCTION

Hello! Welcome to *The Pink Whisk Guide to Cake Making: Brilliant Baking Step-by-Step*. It's full of delicious cake recipes for all sorts of occasions, with helpful step-by-step photos so you know you're on the right track. Some of the recipes started out life on the blog but have all been thoroughly reworked (25 versions of Golden Syrup Cake later…) to make them even more delicious.

This book is not just about the recipes (although of course they do taste great) – it's about making all your cake making even better than before. The pages are loaded with tips and tricks and explanations as to why you should do a certain something at a specific stage – the sort of thing that's missed out of most recipe books. You'll then be able to apply these techniques to all of your cake making – turning you into a Cake Grand Master. They'll be queuing up at the door for a slice!

The book is split into three sections by method; creaming method cakes, whisking method cakes and melting method cakes. There are cakes for everyone and everything. Each recipe also has its own variation – change a bit of this and a bit of that and ta dah! – giving you inspiration to mix up your own flavour combinations.

Don't be frightened of experimenting or using a recipe as the basis for something else. The Ultimate Chocolate Cake, for example, makes an equally good teatime chocolate cake, a chocolate cake for decorating, huge muffins or even cupcakes – the world is your oyster, or the oven is your lobster. Whatever the weather get stuck in and make your cake baking brilliant!

Ruth

x

BAKING EQUIPMENT

Having the right equipment to hand makes baking a piece of cake!

sieve

paper loaf liners

electric hand mixer – speeds up your baking

measuring spoons

baking paper

measuring jug

digital kitchen scales

whisk – a pink one is optional!

mixing spoon

palette knife

silicone spatulas – great for scraping sides of bowls

oven thermometer

Bundt
tin

mixing
bowl

angel cake
mould

baking trays

various round
cake tins

loaf tin

cooling rack

THE BASICS
INGREDIENTS

Baking powder

A raising agent that is a combination of bicarbonate of soda, cream of tartar and cornstarch to absorb moisture. In conjunction with heat and moisture it reacts to form carbon dioxide which makes cakes rise. Cake mixtures made with baking powder don't mind waiting their turn to go into the oven because of this double action. It will stay fresh for about a year but is one of those things that can linger in your cupboard for some time. Be sure to check the best before date!

Bicarbonate of soda (baking soda)

This is used as a raising agent when a recipe contains acid ingredients such as vinegar, yoghurt or soured cream. It relies on the chemical reaction to form carbon dioxide which will give you a light and airy cake. Because the action of bicarbonate of soda is instant, cake mixes using this should go into the oven to be baked straight away after mixing otherwise the gases will escape and the cake won't rise as well.

Self-raising (-rising) flour

A wheat flour which has an added raising agent.

Plain (all-purpose) flour

Finely ground white flour made from wheat grain.

TIP
To turn plain flour into self-raising flour add 25g (1oz) baking powder to every 450g (1lb) plain flour and stir well to distribute it evenly.

Wholemeal (whole-wheat) flour

More nutty in flavour than white flours, wholemeal contains the wheat germ which makes it higher in fibre with a better nutritional content than white flours. It does absorb more moisture so if you're using it in place of a white flour you should also add a little more liquid such as milk.

TIP If brown sugar hardens place it in a small bowl. Fill another small bowl with water and place both in the microwave side by side. Microwave them on full power for 1 minute at a time until the sugar has softened.

Caster (superfine) sugar

Use a caster sugar for baking. It is more finely ground and dissolves into the cake mixture more readily. Granulated sugar can often speckle the top of a cake and can lead to a more crunchy texture.

Muscovado sugars

Brown sugars contain molasses which gives the sugar a soft texture. Light brown sugar has less molasses than a dark sugar and a more delicate toffee type flavour. They should be stored, once opened, in an airtight container to prevent them from hardening. Some brown sugars are referred to as soft light or dark sugar. They are processed slightly differently to a genuine Muscovado sugar and are less rich in taste. They can be used in recipes specifying use of a Muscovado but the depth of flavour will be slightly lessened.

TIP Blitz granulated sugar in the food processor in short 30 second blasts until more finely ground if you run out of caster.

Eggs

Eggs should be used at room temperature, so if you store yours in the fridge make sure you let them come up to room temperature before using. Recipes in the book use large eggs unless otherwise stated, and yes it really does make a difference to the finished product! Large eggs typically weigh between 63g and 73g, medium eggs 53–63g, so by the time you've added 4 eggs to your mix the difference in liquid will make a big difference to your finished cake.

Butter

Butter makes cakes tender and adds colour and flavour. My recipes use a regular salted butter which avoids the need for having to add a pinch of salt. If you do want to use unsalted butter simply add ¼ tsp salt to the cake mixture along with the flour. Butter quickly absorbs flavours so when storing it in the fridge keep it in the coldest area and away from strong-flavoured foods such as onion. Substituting butter for margarine can be done if you prefer but be aware that they often have different water contents which may slightly affect the finished cake.

Chocolate

When buying chocolate for baking it's best to buy either a dark 49% cocoa solids or a 70% cook's chocolate (specifically designed not to split and ruin your finished masterpiece).

TIP To soften butter ready for baking microwave on half power in 30 second bursts until ready to use – but keep your eye on it so it doesn't melt! Alternatively dice the butter and place into a bowl of room temperature water until sufficiently softened, and then drain the water away.

Icing (confectioners) sugar

A super finely ground sugar that can be used to make glazes and icings (frostings) as it dissolves very easily. Icing sugar has a tendency to be slightly lumpy so it's always best to sift it first. Mixing icing sugar with hot, (as opposed to cold) water will also help to avoid getting any lumps!

Cocoa powder

A regular cocoa powder is best for baking. Dutch-processed cocoa is much more expensive and has been treated with an agent that makes it darker in appearance – but as a result it has a milder flavour than regular cocoa powder.

Vanilla extract

This isn't a place for skimping on quality – make sure that you're using an extract derived from vanilla pods, and not a synthetic essence, for the best flavour.

Vanilla bean paste

Vanilla bean paste is brilliant stuff – it's packed with thousands of vanilla bean seeds and means less faffing around splitting and scraping a pod.

> **TIP**
> The reaction between regular cocoa powder and bicarbonate of soda in a recipe darkens the colour and gives it a smoother flavour (e.g. Ultimate Chocolate Cake).

SWEET SUCCESS

Each recipe contains all the techniques for the actual making of the cake but these handy hints can be applied to all your cake making.

Baking is a science…
So it's really important to measure all of your ingredients extremely accurately for good results.

And then comes the oven… I prefer to bake on just one shelf at a time where possible. Loading your oven with cakes makes the temperature drop significantly and they can then take longer to bake through. A shelf positioned a third of the way up from the bottom of the oven is the best place for a cake to bake. The hot air of the oven needs to circulate around the tins for even baking – so don't overload the shelf either, cheeky monkeys! If a tin is too close to the walls or door of the oven then the cake will brown faster on one side than the other.

Most ovens will run slightly hot or slightly cool. If you were cooking a joint of beef it's not going to make a huge difference but in baking a cake things will quickly go wrong. A removable oven thermometer takes out the guesswork and is a great investment if you're baking regularly. Set it on the shelf you plan to bake on and preheat your oven. Read the temperature on the thermometer and then adjust the oven controls until the thermometer shows the correct temperature for your recipe.

It's very difficult to write absolutely precise times for baking; every oven is different and moist ingredients can differ in their water contents. Plan on the 5 minute rule – checking it 5 minutes before bake time is up and then checking every 5 minutes after if it needs a little longer.

When fully baked a cake should be tested by touching with the fingertips – it should be light and springy to the touch. If you insert a skewer into the cake it should come away clean, without any cake mixture sticking to it. If not, it needs a little longer in the oven.

If your cake isn't quite ready you'll see uncooked mixture clinging to your skewer.

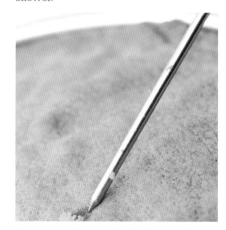
Once the cake is cooked a skewer should come out clean, or with just a few crumbs of cooked cake clinging to it.

Lining a round tin

1 To line a round tin cut a strip of baking (parchment) paper a little larger than the circumference of your tin (all the way around the sides) and approx. 10cm (4in) deep. Make a fold along the long edge, 1.5cm (⅝in) up from the bottom edge, crease well and unfold. Snip at a 45 degree angle from the bottom up to the crease, repeating the snips at 1cm (⅜in) intervals all the way along. The angled snips will help the paper curve around the tin.

2 Now cut a circle of paper for the base of the tin. If you have a loose-bottomed tin, draw around the base and cut out exactly on the line. Otherwise draw around the tin and cut out just inside the line.

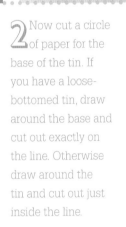

3 Lightly greasing the tin before adding the paper will help it stick in position. Fit the collar around the inside of the tin: the crease should sit directly at the bottom of the tin with the snipped part sitting on the base. Finally add the circle to the base and you're ready to bake.

Lining a loaf tin

1 To line a loaf tin, cut a rectangle 2.5 times the open width and 1.5 times the length.

2 Push the paper into the loaf tin to roughly mark where the bottom corners of the tin are. Remove and cut diagonally from the very corner of the paper to the corner crease mark. Repeat for each of the corners.

TIP

If you bake regularly then having a supply of paper loaf liners and pre-cut baking paper circles is great and will take the faff out of cutting your own!

3 Set the paper into the tin and cut away any excess at the corner folds and around the top. As with round tins, greasing the loaf tin lightly will help the paper stay straight in the tin!

TIP

Greasing sprays, also
know as cake release,
are fairly easy to get
hold of now and make
greasing tricky tins like
Bundts super easy.

Preparing a shaped Bundt tin

It's infuriating when you've baked a
cake and then can't get it out of the tin
(except with a chisel!).

A really good greasing will help when
it comes to turning out a cake and
for shaped tins such as a Bundt it's
important to get into every nook and
cranny. Once baked the cake should be
cooled a little in the tin before turning
out (approx. 30 mins). This allows
the structure of the cake to firm up
so it doesn't fall apart. It should then
be turned out onto a serving plate or
cooling rack and left to cool completely.
Don't leave it to cool fully in the Bundt
tin otherwise it'll never come out!

TROUBLESHOOTING

My cake has come out wonky!

Unevenly risen cakes can happen for a number of reasons. For me it's most likely that the oven shelf isn't level – the first step is to check! They can also rise unevenly if the raising agent (bicarbonate of soda or baking powder) is old and losing it's efficacy or hasn't been dispersed through the cake mixture evenly.

My mixture has curdled…

It's important that all the ingredients are at room temperature when working them together. If the butter or eggs are too cold it can result in a curdled mixture. Add the eggs slowly, beating well after each addition, to allow the mixture to aerate rather than becoming

a liquid sloppy state. Mix, mix, mix is the key to avoiding the dreaded curdle! Adding something very acidic to a cake mix such as lemon juice will cause a curdle. At the end of the day don't worry too much – it's best avoided if you can but if not your cake will still turn out pretty well!

My cake has a volcano effect on top

The oven might have been too hot or the cake too high up in the oven – this can also be the cause of cakes burning on the top. The crust has baked and set before the cake mixture in the centre, and as it bakes through the mixture expands. As it has nowhere else to go it bursts through the top, creating the volcano dome effect. It's a good idea to keep an eye on your cakes whilst baking, peeking through the oven door if you can and if they're beginning to brown too much cover with a sheet of foil for the remaining baking time, or dropping the oven temperature just slightly. Domed cakes can generally be rescued by slicing off the top and disguising with icing.

My cake top has a crunchy 'skin'

This will happen if the butter and sugar weren't worked into the cake mixture

well enough. The butter and sugar can end up on the top of the cake as you scrape the bowl clean of cake mixture. Make sure your mixture is thoroughly even before filling your cake tin.

Disaster! My cake has sunk in the middle

Cakes sink when they have too little flour or too many eggs in the mixture so it's important to check and weigh your ingredients correctly. Avoid opening the oven door whilst baking as the draught and sudden temperature drop caused by doing so can cause a flop!

All the fruit has sunk in my cake

Fruit will sink if the cake mixture is too wet. Make sure the fruit isn't in huge pieces as the weight of them will cause them to sink. Make sure the pieces are dry and toss them in a tablespoon of flour before adding to the cake mix. To reduce the wetness of a cake mixture make sure you are using the size of eggs stated in the recipe.

How big is my loaf tin?

Unfortunately manufacturers have yet to standardise loaf tin sizes which can make life a little tricky sussing out the capacity of your tin A good way to check is to measure how much water your tin will hold. A 900g (2lb) loaf tin will hold just over 1 litre (36fl oz) of water and a 450g (1lb) loaf tin will hold just over 500ml (18fl oz) so you will know if your tin is suitable for a certain recipe or not. Just remember that if your tin is very deep, or very shallow, then you will need to keep a good eye on the baking time and put all your 'testing for doneness' skills to good use!

USING UP EGGS

It always seems such a waste to be left with egg yolks or whites at the end of a recipe and not have anything to do with them. Here's how to use them for custard or meringues – always useful and delicious!

Meringue – Whites

Whites	Sugar (grams)
1	55
2	110
3	165
4	220
5	275
6	330
7	385
8	440
9	495
10	550

1 Whisk the egg whites until they start to look foamy. Continue whisking, adding the sugar 1 spoonful at a time, allowing each to be whisked in before adding the next until all the sugar has been added.

2 Whisk until the whites stand in firm peaks. Pipe or shape your meringues and bake in the oven at 120°C (fan)/140°C/275°F/Gas Mark 1 for 1½ –2 hours for a Pavlova and 1 hour for smaller meringues.

Custard – Yolks

Yolks	Milk (ml)	Cream (ml)	Sugar (grams)
1	30	40	15
2	60	80	30
3	90	115	45
4	125	150	60
5	155	190	75
6	185	230	90
7	215	265	105
8	250	305	120
9	280	340	135
10	310	380	150

1 Whisk together the egg yolks and caster (superfine) sugar in a large jug and set to one side.

2 Heat the milk and cream gently until just below boiling point. Whilst whisking continuously, pour the milk/cream slowly over the egg yolks and sugar until they are well mixed together.

3 Return the mixture to the pan and heat gently, stirring continuously to prevent the egg from scrambling, until the mixture thickens enough to coat the back of a spoon.

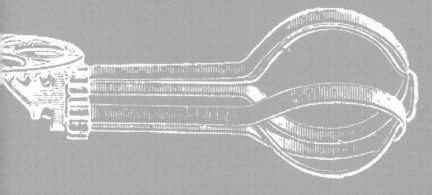

CREAMING METHOD

Creaming method cakes are made by beating sugar into butter until light and fluffy. The creamed mixture should almost double in volume and will go very pale. Time spent getting this stage just right and incorporating lots of air is the foundation for any super-soft and light cake.

VICTORIA SPONGE

* *

MAKES ONE 20CM (8IN) CAKE
PREP ⏱ 25 MINUTES PLUS COOLING | BAKE ⏱ 30 MINUTES
OVEN 160°C (FAN)/180°C/350°F/GAS MARK 4

The perfect Victoria sponge seems to be the holy grail of baking – if you can achieve a well-risen, golden, fluffy sponge you can conquer anything! There are a couple of tricks to help you on the way: the creaming of the butter and sugar and good-quality tins. Follow the steps and you'll soon be the grand master of fabulous sponge cakes.

INGREDIENTS

Cake
250g (9oz) very soft butter,
    plus a little extra for greasing
250g (9oz) caster (superfine) sugar
1 tsp vanilla extract
4 eggs, large
250g (9oz) self-raising (-rising) flour
2 tbsp milk

Filling
200ml (7fl oz) double (heavy) cream
2 tbsp icing (confectioners) sugar
1 tsp vanilla bean paste or the seeds
    from inside 1 vanilla pod
225g (8oz) seedless raspberry jam

A little icing (confectioners) sugar
    to dust

EQUIPMENT
2 x 20cm (8in) round sandwich tins
    (layer cake pans)
Baking (parchment) paper
Electric hand-held whisk or food
    mixer
Piping bag fitted with 1cm (⅜ in)
    round nozzle (optional)
Icing sugar sifter

1 Preheat the oven to 160°C (fan) / 180°C / 350°F / Gas Mark 4. Prepare the cake tins by greasing them well and lining the base of each with a circle of baking paper.

TIP **Good quality tins are one of the keys to the perfect cake – they distribute the heat evenly allowing the cake to rise evenly as it bakes, avoiding the domed top effect.**

2 Before you cream the butter and sugar together, the butter needs to be really softened – take no shortcuts here. You should be able to easily push a knife right through the block of butter with little to no resistance. Dice and put it into a microwave-proof bowl and heat for 30 seconds in the microwave on half power if it's not soft enough – but don't let it melt!

3 Place the butter in a large bowl and add the caster sugar. Using an electric hand whisk begin to cream them together. Keep going until the mixture has gone very pale: it should almost double in volume and you should no longer feel the texture of the sugar within the butter. This will take you 5–6 minutes. It's worth the effort – the air you incorporate now will result in a lovely fluffy sponge.

4 Add the vanilla extract to the creamed butter and sugar and stir together. Crack the eggs into a jug and beat them with a fork so that they are less likely to curdle when added to the creamed butter and sugar.

5 Add a small amount of the beaten eggs, just a little drop, and whisk them in fully. Add another drop and beat again. As you add more and more egg the mixture will slip about as you whisk it – but keep whisking until the egg and the creamed butter and sugar come together. It's really important to do it step by step and whisk the air back into the mixture before adding the next drop of egg. Keep working this way until all of the egg is incorporated and you have a light and fluffy mixture – still packed with the air bubbles you've been working in (and not a sign of curdling!). If the air isn't worked back in after each addition the mix will be very liquidy and will have lost all the oomph you gave it in the creaming stage. For the best cakes it's worth spending the time doing it slowly.

6 Now comes the flour. Prepare to be shocked: I don't sift it! I've found it makes little to no difference in the finished result. However, if your flour has been sitting in the cupboard for a fair while and is looking lumpy, it will need sifting in. Set aside the electric mixer and add the flour to the butter, sugar and egg mixture in the bowl. Using a thin edged spatula or a metal spoon fold in the flour, cutting through the mixture, lifting and turning it until all of the flour is incorporated. Add the milk and stir through.

7 Divide the mixture evenly between the two tins and roughly level with the back of spoon. Try to avoid getting mixture up the sides of the tins if you can as this can give the finished cakes a little raised lip.

TIP Turn out onto a plate first and then onto a cooling rack so that they go onto the cooling rack base down, otherwise you'll end up with criss cross marks across the top of your cake.

8 Bake in the oven for 25–30 minutes until golden brown and when pressed lightly on the top the cakes spring back up. Allow to cool in the tins for 5 minutes before removing and cooling fully on a wire rack. If left in tins to cool completely cakes will 'sweat' and become soggy. It's fine to leave the paper on the bases as they cool.

9 Once fully cooled it's time to assemble the cake. Place the cream, icing sugar and vanilla bean paste in a large bowl. Whisk until the cream forms soft peaks. Set to one side.

10 Remove the paper from the base of each cake and choose which will be the top, setting this one to one side. Place the base cake onto a serving plate and cover with a generous layer of raspberry jam. Don't take the jam right up to the edge of the cake, but about 1cm (⅜in) away from the edge all the way round.

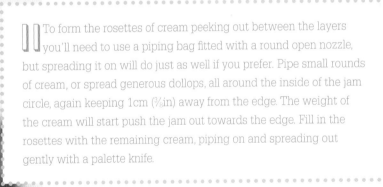

11 To form the rosettes of cream peeking out between the layers you'll need to use a piping bag fitted with a round open nozzle, but spreading it on will do just as well if you prefer. Pipe small rounds of cream, or spread generous dollops, all around the inside of the jam circle, again keeping 1cm (⅜in) away from the edge. The weight of the cream will start push the jam out towards the edge. Fill in the rosettes with the remaining cream, piping on and spreading out gently with a palette knife.

12 Carefully lift the top of the cake into position. The weight of it will squidge out the jam and cream so that it just sits at the edge of the cake. Dust with a little icing sugar and ta dah! Perfect Victoria sponge.

TIP Not feeling quite so lavish? Skip the cream and go with the jam!

COFFEE-FLAVOURED VICTORIA SPONGE

Flavouring plain cakes is extremely easy with the wealth of extracts that can be bought in the supermarket, or by using dissolved coffee granules as here. Always add your flavouring to the creamed butter and sugar – the fat traps the flavour and distributes it evenly throughout your cake.

QUANTITY: MAKES ONE 20 CM (8 IN) CAKE
PREP ⏱ 25 MINUTES PLUS COOLING | BAKE ⏱ 30 MINUTES
OVEN 160°C (FAN)/180°C/350°F/GAS MARK 4

TIP
To make your own flavoured sugar take a jar with a tight-fitting lid and fill it three quarters full of caster sugar. Add cinnamon sticks, a tablespoon of dried lavender or cardamom pods. Screw on the lid and shake it up. Allow to infuse in the cupboard for two weeks before using in your cakes.

INGREDIENTS
Cake
250g (9oz) very soft butter, plus a little extra for greasing
250g (9oz) caster (superfine) sugar
1 tsp instant coffee, dissolved in 2 tbsp boiling water
4 eggs, large
250g (9oz) self-raising (-rising) flour

Filling
200ml (7fl oz) double (heavy) cream
2 tbsp icing (confectioners) sugar
1 tsp instant coffee, dissolved in 2tbsp boiling water.

A little icing (confectioners) sugar to dust

EQUIPMENT
2 x 20cm (8in) round sandwich tins (layer cake pans)
Baking (parchment) paper
Electric hand-held whisk or food mixer
Piping bag fitted with 1cm (⅜in) round nozzle (optional)
Icing sugar sifter

1 Follow the same method as Victoria Sponge, but omit the vanilla extract and add the coffee flavouring (1 tsp instant coffee dissolved in 2 tbsp boiling water) by whisking it into the creamed butter and sugar, before adding the eggs.

2 For the filling make yourself some coffee cream by placing all the filling ingredients in a bowl and whisking to soft peaks. Use just as the cream in the Victoria Sponge recipe.

CHERRY MADEIRA

· ·

MAKES ONE 900G (2LB) LOAF CAKE
PREP ⏱ 30 MINUTES PLUS COOLING | BAKE ⏱ 50 MINUTES
OVEN 160°C (FAN)/180°C/350°F/GAS MARK 4

Finally a recipe that doesn't have all the cherries sunk at the bottom of the cake – because they are cut into quarters first. Once you're slicing this beauty not a single person will say the pieces of cherry aren't big enough (however, when someone asks for 'that cake with all the cherries at the bottom' feel free to give them a clip round the ear!).

INGREDIENTS
Cake
250g (9oz) glacé (candied) cherries
150ml (5fl oz) beaten eggs
   (3 medium)
150g (5½oz) butter, softened
150g (5½oz) caster (superfine) sugar
130g (4½oz) plain (all-purpose) flour
50g (1¾oz) self-raising (-rising) flour

To decorate
50g (1¾oz) icing (confectioners)
   sugar, sifted
1–2 tsp hot water

EQUIPMENT
Electric handmixer or stand mixer
900g (2lb) loaf tin (pan),
   18.5 x 11.5cm (7 x 4½in)

1 Preheat the oven to 160°C (fan)/180°C/350°F/Gas Mark 4, and line the loaf tin with baking paper.

2 Quarter each glacé cherry with a sharp knife. Not halves, not wholes, they won't stay up up up! Place the quartered cherries in a sieve over a bowl and pour boiling water over them. Allow them to stand for a minute before swishing round to wash them free of any syrupy juice. Tip the cherries onto a couple of sheets of kitchen paper – spacing them out and patting them dry. Put them into a dry bowl and set to one side.

3 Now for the eggs, 3 medium eggs are called for here. Crack them into a jug and beat the yolks and whites together with a fork. You need 150ml (5fl oz) of beaten egg and not a drop more. Controlling the liquid content will keep those cherries suspended in the cake mixture, so drain out a little of the beaten egg until you have exactly the right amount. Now on with the cake!

4 Cream together the butter and sugar – nice and light and fluffy please. Beat in the vanilla extract, then start to add the egg a little at a time and beat well after each addition until it's fully incorporated.

5 Weigh out the flours and add one tablespoon to the cherries. Toss the cherries and flour together until they are all lightly coated.

6 Add the rest of the flour and the coated cherries to the cake mixture and fold together using a spatula until the cake mixture is nice and even.

7 Scrape down the sides of the bowl to make sure the cherries are evenly dispersed before spooning the mixture into the loaf tin. Roughly level with the back of spoon and bake in the oven for 50 minutes. Test the cake by inserting a skewer – it should come out clean. If there is still moist cake mixture stuck to it then bake for a further 5 minutes and test again.

TIP Quartering the cherries before rinsing means that the syrup hiding in the middle gets washed away too. If left in the syrup the cherries will most certainly make a beeline for the bottom of the cake!

8 Remove from the oven and allow to cool fully on a wire rack. Once cooled, mix the sifted icing sugar with a little hot water to make an icing with a thick consistency. Drizzle over the top of the cake and serve.

CHOC CHIP & FUDGE MADEIRA

Naturally this is a firm hit with the children and is the slice most regularly requested as a treat in lunchboxes! Any combination of milk, dark and white chips work well – or throw in your own favourite additions.

MAKES ONE 900G (2LB) LOAF CAKE
PREP ⏱ 25 MINUTES PLUS COOLING | BAKE ⏱ 50 MINUTES
OVEN 160°C (FAN)/180°C/350°F/GAS MARK 4

INGREDIENTS
Cake
150g (5½oz) butter, softened
150g (5½oz) caster (superfine) sugar
150ml (5fl oz) beaten eggs (3 medium)
130g (4½oz) plain (all-purpose) flour
50g (1¾oz) self-raising (-rising) flour
100g (3½oz) dark chocolate chips
50g (1¾oz) fudge chunks

To decorate
25g (1oz) dark chocolate chips, melted
20g (¾oz) fudge chunks

EQUIPMENT
Electric handmixer or stand mixer
900g (2lb) loaf tin (pan), 18.5 x 11.5cm (7 x 4½in)

1 Follow the same method as the Cherry Madeira, except choc chips and fudge chunks need no washing and chopping so toss them in a tablespoon of the flour and you're ready to go.

2 Drizzle the finished cake with melted chocolate and scatter on the fudge chunks. Serve.

TIP
Tossing the choc chips and fudge in a little of the flour helps to give the cake mixture something to grip onto and keeps them up where they should be rather than skulking at the bottom!

COCONUT & PASSIONFRUIT BUNDT

· ·

MAKES ONE 25CM (10IN) BUNDT CAKE
PREP ⏱ 25 MINUTES PLUS COOLING | BAKE ⏱ 35 MINUTES
OVEN 160°C (FAN)/180°C/350°F/GAS MARK 4

This is an unassuming cake in the looks department, but you'll definitely be going back for more! The crunchy seeds of the passionfruit are lovely, but if you'd prefer your cake without them simply push the pulp of the passionfruit through a sieve and discard the seeds.

INGREDIENTS

Cake
250g (9oz) very soft butter
265g (9½oz) caster (superfine) sugar
4 eggs, large
200g (7oz) self-raising (-rising) flour
Pulp from 2 large passionfruit,
    approx. 80g (3oz) each
100g (3½oz) creamed coconut,
    finely grated
140ml (4½fl oz) coconut cream

To decorate
50g (1¾oz) icing (confectioners)
    sugar, sifted
2 tsp coconut cream

EQUIPMENT
2.4 l (12 cup) Bundt tin (Bundt pan)
Electric hand-held whisk or
    food mixer
Disposable plastic piping bag

1 Preheat the oven to 160°C(fan)/180°C/350°F/Gas Mark 4. Prepare the tin: grease it well, including the ring in the centre and all the other little nooks and crannies.

TIP Cake release spray is a handy little helper when it comes to tricky shaped tins that can't be lined with paper. A good generous spray takes the hard work out of greasing tins.

2 Cream together the butter and sugar until pale and fluffy using an electric whisk or food mixer.

3 Beat the eggs together in a separate jug. Add the beaten eggs a tiny little bit at a time to the butter and sugar mixture, beating in well after each addition.

4 Add the flour to the bowl and fold through using a spatula or metal spoon. Scrape the pulp from the passionfruit and add to the bowl, along with the finely grated creamed coconut and the coconut cream. Fold through until evenly distributed through out the mixture.

5 Fill the prepared Bundt tin with the mixture, dolloping it into the base of the tin to form a ring. Gently smooth over the surface with the back of a spoon so it sits evenly.

TIP This recipe will fit into a smaller 2.1l (9 cup) Bundt tin if you prefer – you'll just have a slightly taller cake!

6 Bake in the preheated oven for 35 minutes. Insert a metal skewer through a crack in the top of the cake to see if it's done – it should come out clean or with just a few moist crumbs. If there is still cake mixture clinging to it bob it back into the oven and check at five-minute intervals until cooked all the way through.

7 Once baked you need to negotiate getting it out of the tin in one piece. First up let it cool, in the tin, for 30 minutes. This allows the structure of the cake to firm up – flip it out straight from the oven and it'll come out in bits! Once you've let it cool take a plate and place it over the top of the tin, and in one swift movement flip it over. The cake should drop down directly onto the plate. Remove the tin and allow the cake to cool down fully.

8 Sift the icing sugar into a bowl and add 2 teaspoons of coconut cream. Mix it up to a fairly stiff icing – it should be the same consistency as a thick custard. If it's too thick add a little water but only a tiny bit at a time. Fill the piping bag with the coconut icing and set to one side.

9 Transfer the cake carefully to a serving plate. Taking a long strip of cling film (plastic wrap), wrap it around the edge of the plate tucking it neatly against the bottom edge of the cake. This will stop the plate being covered in flicks of icing. Snip the end off the piping bag and drizzle the icing all the way round the cake. Remove the cling film from the plate and serve.

RASPBERRY & WHITE CHOCOLATE BUNDT

Raspberry and white chocolate is a classic combination that works a treat in this Bundt cake. Of course you could use your favourite fruits as an alternative, but watch out for strawberries – they aren't ideal for use in baking as they have such a high proportion of water. Try blackberries, forest fruits and blueberries instead!

MAKES ONE 30CM (12IN) BUNDT CAKE
PREP ⏲ 25 MINUTES PLUS COOLING | BAKE ⏲ 35 MINUTES
OVEN 160°C (FAN)/180°C/350°F/GAS MARK 4

INGREDIENTS:

Cake

265g (9½oz) caster (superfine) sugar
4 eggs, large
200g (7oz) self-raising (-rising) flour
140g (5oz) raspberries

To decorate

20g (¾oz) raspberries
50g (1¾oz) icing (confectioners) sugar

EQUIPMENT

2.4 l (12 cup) Bundt tin (Bundt pan)
Electric hand-held whisk or food mixer
Fine sieve
Disposable plastic piping bag

1 Follow the same method as Coconut & Passionfruit Bundt, but omit the grated creamed coconut, passionfruit and coconut cream and replace instead with raspberries and grated white chocolate.

2 For the icing push the raspberries through a sieve and discard the seeds. Mix the sieved pulp with the icing sugar, adding a little water if necessary, and then drizzle over the Bundt cake.

CINNAMON PECAN 'CUPPA' CAKE

MAKES ONE 20CM (8IN) SQUARE CAKE
PREP ⏱ 25 MINUTES PLUS COOLING | BAKE ⏱ 55 MINUTES
OVEN 160°C (FAN)/180°C/350°F/GAS MARK 4

Traditionally this type of cake was called a coffee cake, not that it's coffee flavoured but because it's a deliciously moist cake ideal for eating with your morning coffee. Whatever your mid-morning tipple, a slice of this beauty will go down a treat!

INGREDIENTS

Filling

100g (3½oz) butter
2tsp ground cinnamon
60g (2¼oz) soft light brown sugar
100g (3½oz) pecans, chopped

Cake

100g (3½oz) butter
200g (7oz) caster (superfine) sugar
2 eggs, large
230ml (8fl oz) Greek-style yoghurt
185g (6½oz) plain (all-purpose) flour
½ tsp bicarbonate of soda

EQUIPMENT

20cm (8in) square cake tin (pan),
 at least 7.5cm (3in) deep
Electric handmixer

1 Preheat the oven to 160°C (fan)/180°C/350°F/ Gas Mark 4. Prepare the filling: place the butter, cinnamon and light brown sugar in a small bowl and mash together with a fork. Roughly chop the pecans, add to the mixture and mix it up well. Set it to one side and get to work on the cake.

2 Line the tin with baking paper. Cream together the butter and sugar until light and fluffy. It's harder to do when the ratio of butter and sugar isn't even – keep going, it just takes a bit longer.

3 Add the egg a little at a time and beat well until the mixture is fluffy and aerated again, repeating until all the egg is incorporated. Getting the aeration back in after adding the egg is super important otherwise you'll just have a liquidy mixture that turns very dense when baked.

4 Add the flour, bicarbonate of soda and the Greek-style yoghurt. Fold the mixture together with a spatula until evenly combined. Place half of the cake mixture into the base of the tin and spread evenly with the back of a spoon. It will seem like a small amount – don't worry.

5 Now it's messy fingers time! Using half of the filling pinch off small clumps and dot over the cake mixture.

TIP Greek-style yoghurt is lower in fat than soured cream which is why I'm using it here – go for the full fat soured cream if you have it or use plain natural yoghurt instead. Measure these by volume and not by weight.

6 On top dot spoonfuls of the remaining cake mixture to cover the filling. Use up all the remaining cake mixture and then using the back of a spoon smooth the cake mixture together to cover up the filling completely.

7 Dot the remaining filling onto the top of the cake and bake in the oven for 55 minutes until dark golden brown.

TIP Because bicarbonate of soda is the raising agent in the cake here it needs to go in the oven pretty sharpish.

8 Allow to cool in the tin for 10 minutes before transferring to a wire rack to cool completely. Store in an airtight tin and serve with your mid-morning cuppa!

JAM BAKEWELL 'CUPPA' CAKE

A very British twist on an American classic – still as deliciously lovely with your morning brew!

QUANTITY: MAKES ONE 20 CM (8 IN) SQUARE CAKE
PREP ⏱ 25 MINUTES PLUS COOLING | BAKE ⏱ 50 MINUTES
OVEN 160°C (FAN)/180°C/350°F/GAS MARK 4

1 First mix together the bakewell filling – beating together the caster sugar, melted butter, ground almonds, semolina, egg and almond extract. Set aside.

2 For the cake follow the same method as the Cinnamon Pecan cake. Add half the cake mixture to the tin. Dot on top small teaspoonsful of jam and spread together gently with the back of the spoon. Now dot on all of the bakewell mixture in the same way and spread together.

3 Top with the remaining half of the cake mixture, level roughly with the back of a spoon and scatter the flaked almonds on top.

4 Bake for 50 minutes until golden brown. Allow to cool for 10 minutes in the tin before transferring to a wire rack to cool completely. Serve.

INGREDIENTS

Filling

50g (1¾oz) caster (superfine) sugar

50g (1¾oz) melted butter

50g (1¾oz) ground almonds

50g (1¾oz) semolina

1 egg, large

½ tsp almond extract

170g (6oz) raspberry jam (about half an average-sized jar)

Cake

100g (3½oz) butter

200g (7oz) caster (superfine) sugar

2 eggs, large

230ml (8 fl oz) Greek-style yoghurt

185g (6½oz) plain (all-purpose) flour

½ tsp bicarbonate of soda

To decorate

30g (1oz) flaked almonds

EQUIPMENT

20cm (8in) square cake tin (pan), at least 7.5cm (3in) deep
Electric handmixer

TIP The semolina adds a little bit of crunch to the proceedings – if you don't have any double the quantity of ground almonds instead.

LEMON & ELDERFLOWER DRIZZLE CAKE

MAKES ONE 900G (2LB) LOAF CAKE
PREP ⏰ 20 MINUTES PLUS COOLING | BAKE ⏰ 50 MINUTES
OVEN 160°C (FAN)/180°C/350°F/GAS MARK 4

With a crunchy elderflower topping this cake is a little treasure – bursting with zesty sunshine flavour!

INGREDIENTS
Cake
175g (6oz) butter
175g (6oz) caster (superfine) sugar
Zest of 2 lemons,
3 eggs, large
160g (5¾oz) self-raising
   (-rising) flour
Juice of 1 lemon

Drizzle
Juice of 1 lemon
2 tbsp elderflower cordial
110g (4oz) caster (superfine) sugar

EQUIPMENT
900g (2lb) loaf tin (pan),
   18.5 x 11.5cm (7 x 4½in)
Electric handmixer
Juicer
Zester or small grater

1 Preheat the oven to 160°C (fan)/180°C/350°F/ Gas Mark 4. Line the loaf tin with baking paper or a paper liner.

2 Cream together the butter and sugar until light and fluffy. Add the lemon zest and mix until evenly combined. Add the eggs a little at a time, beating well after each addition until the mixture is light and fluffy again.

4 Finally stir through the juice of 1 lemon – don't worry if the mixture curdles, the acidity from the lemon juice will often do that.

3 Fold in the self-raising flour until the cake mix is even.

5 Fill the loaf tin with cake mixture. Level the top roughly with the back of a spoon and bake in the oven for 50 minutes. Do check the oven after 35 minutes and if the crust is going very dark cover it with a sheet of foil for the remaining baking time.

6 Remove the cake from the oven and mix together the drizzle – lemon juice, elderflower cordial and sugar, stirring well to combine. The sugar will still be granular in the mixture.

TIP

The topping is designed to be crunchy – if you don't fancy the crunch heat the drizzle gently in a small pan until the syrup clears and then pour slowly over the skewered cake.

7 Keep the cake in the tin and using a skewer prick holes right across and all round the top of the cake – aim to go three quarters of the way through the cake, not right to the base. Lots of holes are needed for the syrup to soak the cake evenly.

8 Now spoon the drizzle over the top of the cake slowly, allowing it to run down the skewered holes before adding another spoonful. Make sure you evenly cover the entire top of the cake until all the drizzle has been added. Set aside for the cake to cool completely and then remove from the tin and serve.

GINGER & LIME DRIZZLE CAKE

A fiery, zesty version of this cake but any combination of citrus fruits work well in a drizzle cake – why not try orange, lemon and lime?

MAKES ONE 900G (2LB) LOAF CAKE
PREP ⏱ 20 MINUTES PLUS COOLING | BAKE ⏱ 50 MINUTES
OVEN 160°C (FAN)/180°C/350°F/GAS MARK 4

1 Follow the same method as Lemon and Elderflower Drizzle Cake, but add the zest of a lime, 2 diced stem ginger pieces and 1 tsp stem ginger syrup to the creamed butter and sugar. Add 2 teaspoons of ground ginger along with the flour.

2 Once the cake mixture is made, stir through the juice of 1 lime. Bake in the oven for 50 minutes until golden brown.

3 Mix up the drizzle using the juice of 1 lime, stem ginger syrup and caster sugar. Spoon over the skewered cake and allow to cool in the tin before serving.

INGREDIENTS
Cake
175g (6oz) butter
175g (6oz) caster (superfine) sugar
Zest of 1 lime
2 pieces of stem ginger, finely diced
1 tsp stem ginger syrup
3 eggs, large
160g (5¾oz) self-raising (-rising) flour
2 tsp ground ginger
Juice of 1 lime

Drizzle
Juice of 1 lime
20ml stem ginger syrup
100g (3½oz) caster (superfine) sugar

EQUIPMENT
900g (2lb) loaf tin (pan), 18.5 x 11.5cm (7 x 4½in)
Electric handmixer
Juicer
Zester or small grater

TIP If you fancy your drizzle with extra crunch try using granulated sugar instead.

ULTIMATE CHOCOLATE CAKE

MAKES ONE 20CM (8IN) CAKE
PREP ⏱ 1 HOUR 30 MINUTES PLUS COOLING
BAKE ⏱ 1 HOUR 10 MINUTES
OVEN 160°C (FAN)/180°C/350°F/GAS MARK 4

A showstopper for a grand occasion! If you need a go-to chocolate cake recipe then this is your one. It's equally good with a chocolate icing for a teatime treat as it is dressed up to the nines here for special occasions.

INGREDIENTS

Cake
220ml (8fl oz) milk
2 tbsp malt vinegar
165g (6oz) butter, softened
330g (11½oz) light Muscovado sugar
3 eggs, large
200g (7oz) plain (all-purpose) flour
60g (2¼oz) self-raising (-rising) flour
70g (2½oz) cocoa powder
1 tsp bicarbonate of soda

Ganache
275ml (9½ fl oz) double (heavy) cream
1 tbsp golden (corn) syrup
350g (12oz) dark (bittersweet) chocolate, roughly chopped

Buttercream
400g (14oz) icing (confectioners) sugar, sifted
200g (7oz) butter, softened
175g (6oz) white chocolate, melted
3 tbsp double (heavy) cream

Decoration
Large milk chocolate stars
50g (1¾oz) dark chocolate chips
50g (1¾oz) white chocolate chips

EQUIPMENT
20cm (8in) cake tin (pan), at least 7.5cm (3in) deep
Cling film (plastic wrap)
Long serrated knife
Serving plate, at least 23cm (9in) wide

1 Preheat the oven to 160°C (fan)/180°C/350°F/Gas Mark 4. Line the base and sides of the cake tin.

2 Measure the milk into a jug and add the malt vinegar. Give it a quick stir and set to one side.

TIP The vinegar added to the milk creates a crude form of buttermilk, which can be difficult to get hold of. This combination creates just the right acidity to work with the bicarbonate of soda. Similarly natural yoghurt would work a treat too.

3 Cream together the butter and sugar: take your time to get it super light and fluffy. Add the eggs a little drop at a time, beating well after each addition, working the air back into the mixture.

4 You're going to have to sift the cocoa powder to get the lumps out so you might as well sift in the plain and self-raising and the bicarbonate of soda too.

5 Pour in the milk/vinegar mixture and stir together, working in the milk mixture and folding in the flour. Don't beat too vigorously at this stage or the flour will work large air bubbles into the mixture resulting in holes in your cake.

6 Transfer the mixture into the prepared tin and level roughly with the back of a spoon. Bake in the preheated oven for 1 hour 10 minutes. Check it after 50 minutes and cover with foil if the top is browning too much. Once baked leave to cool a little in the tin before transferring to a wire rack to cool completely.

7 Time to prepare the ganache. Place the cream and golden syrup in a pan and heat over a gentle heat until just below boiling point. Remove from the heat and tip in the chopped chocolate. Allow it to stand for two minutes and then gently stir together into a smooth glossy ganache. Transfer to a clean bowl and allow to cool to room temperature. This can take up to 4 hours so prepare your ganache as soon as the cake goes in the oven and then you won't be waiting around for it.

8 For the buttercream, beat together the sifted icing sugar and butter until it's light and airy. It will go very pale and increase greatly in volume. Melt the white chocolate and allow to cool a little (if you add it to the buttercream whilst it's red hot the buttercream will start to melt). Once the chocolate is cool, but still liquid, beat it into the buttercream along with the double cream and set to one side.

9 Once the cake has cooled fully wrap it tightly in cling film and chill it in the fridge for 1 hour. Once chilled, unwrap the cake and slice away the domed top using a sharp serrated knife. Cut the cake into three equal layers, working carefully through the cake with the serrated knife. Scoring first around the cake in the required cutting position will help prevent the cake disintegrating into crumbs.

TIP Chilled cake is much easier to split into layers than room temperature cake. Wrapping it well in cling film is a must otherwise the cake will dry out.

10 Put the three layers back together and turn the cake over and onto a board or large, flat plate (something you can prepare the cake on) so that the flat bottom now becomes the top.

11 Remove the top two layers and spread a quarter of the buttercream over the surface of the bottom layer. Lift layer 2 into position on top of the buttercream. Spread another quarter of the buttercream over the top and place the top of the cake back into position. Apply a thin layer of buttercream to the top of the cake.

12 Start working around the sides, covering the cake completely in a thin, even layer of buttercream. Smooth the buttercream with a palette knife. Once the sides are covered turn your attention back to the top, smoothing together with the sides and levelling off any uneven places. Don't be afraid to almost scrape off the buttercream with the palette knife in areas where it's a little too heavy, working around the cake until it's as even as you can get it. Now it needs to go back into the fridge to chill for half an hour until the buttercream firms up.

13 Prepare your serving plate: cut six strips of baking paper approximately 13cm x 5cm (5in x 2in) and position onto the serving plate, overlapping to form a rough circle where the edge of the cake will be.

14 Cut away any excess buttercream at the base of the chilled cake and carefully transfer it onto the serving plate, lifting carefully with a palette knife. Adjust the slips of baking paper so that they sit half way under the cake and completely shield the serving plate. These slips stop the plate getting messy with dribbling ganache and will be whipped away at the end!

15 Now for the ganache. It should be cooled to room temperature and be the perfect spreadable consistency. If yours has set too firm warm it very gently in the microwave on half power for 30 seconds. Using a clean palette knife apply a good coating to the top of the cake. Turn your attention to the sides, applying more ganache and smoothing it out – be sure to reach from the top of the cake to the very bottom edge. Once you've worked all the way around the outside of the cake go back to the top of the cake, where there will be a lip around the outside edge created by coating the sides. Using the palette knife knock this gently back in and smooth the top again. Check the sides for any thin spots of ganache where the buttercream peeks through and apply extra dots of ganache to cover, smoothing as you go.

16 Once you're happy with the finish decorate the top with large milk chocolate stars and a scattering of dark and white chocolate chips. Run a sharp knife around the base of the cake and slip out the baking paper protecting the plate. Serve!

TIRAMISU CAKE

Turn the Ultimate Chocolate Cake into a Tiramisu-flavoured cake by following these quick and easy steps.

MAKES ONE 20 CM (8 IN) CAKE
PREP ⏱ 1 HOUR 30 MINUTES PLUS COOLING
BAKE ⏱ 1 HOUR 10 MINUTES
OVEN 160°C (FAN)/180°C/350°F/GAS MARK 4

1 Follow the same method as Ultimate Chocolate Cake, but add to the creamed butter and sugar 1tsp of instant coffee dissolved in 1 tbsp hot water before beating in the eggs to make the cake a mocha flavour instead.

2 For the buttercream omit the double cream and melted white chocolate, instead beating in 1 tbsp marsala wine and 1 tsp instant coffee dissolved in 1 tbsp of hot water.

3 The ganache is made using a combination of dark chocolate and cappuccino flavoured buttons (see suppliers).

4 Assemble the cake in the same way but decorate with chocolate covered coffee beans, white chocolate chips and chopped cappuccino buttons.

INGREDIENTS

Cake
220ml milk
2 tbsp malt vinegar
165g (6oz) butter, softened
330g (11½oz) light muscovado sugar
1 tsp instant coffee dissolved in 1 tbsp hot water
3 eggs, large
200g (7oz) plain (all-purpose) flour
60g (2¼oz) self-raising (-rising) flour
70g (2½oz) cocoa powder
1 tsp bicarbonate of soda

Buttercream
200g (7oz) butter, softened
400g (14oz) icing (confectioners) sugar, sifted
1 tbsp marsala wine
1 tsp instant coffee dissolved in 1 tbsp hot water

Ganache
275ml (9½fl oz) double (heavy) cream
1 tbsp golden (corn) syrup
150g (5½oz) dark chocolate
200g (7oz) cappuccino flavoured chocolate buttons

Decoration
Chocolate coated coffee beans
50g (1¾oz) white chocolate chips
50g (1¾oz) cappuccino buttons

EQUIPMENT
20cm (8in) cake tin (pan), at least 7.5cm (3in) deep
Cling film (plastic wrap)
Long serrated knife
Serving plate, at least 23cm (9in) wide

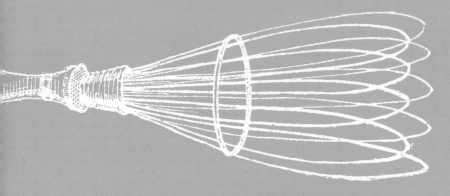

WHISKING METHOD

Beaten eggs are the key to successful cakes in this category – either whisking whole eggs with sugar or beating egg whites to incorporate the air for your cake. They need a gentle touch to retain as much air as possible but are well worth the effort!

SWISS ROLL

. . . .

MAKES ONE SWISS ROLL
PREP ⏰ 25 MINUTES PLUS COOLING | BAKE ⏰ 15 MINUTES
OVEN 160°C (FAN)/180°C/350°F/GAS MARK 4

I don't think you can beat the taste of a freshly made Swiss Roll.
Believe me, they are a cinch to make and nothing to be afraid of.
There's no fat added in the form of butter, so if kept a Swiss Roll
will stale quickly – not much chance of that in my house! Don't let
the lack of a Swiss Roll tin put you off – baking or roasting trays are
often just the right size.

INGREDIENTS
Cake

4 eggs, large
100g (3½oz) caster (superfine) sugar
100g (3½oz) plain (all-purpose) flour

Filling and rolling

A little caster (superfine) sugar for
   rolling
175g (6oz) raspberry jam (about half
   an average-sized jar)

EQUIPMENT

Electric handmixer
Swiss Roll tin (pan) or shallow-sided
   roasting tray approx. 33 x 23cm
   (13 x 9in)
Spreader

TIP Greasing the tin before lining with paper will help stick and mould the paper to the tin – otherwise it'll keep jumping out at you!

1 Preheat the oven to 160°C (fan)/180°C/350°F/Gas Mark 4. Grease the tin and cut a piece of baking paper about 3cm (1¼in) larger than the tin all the way around. Push the paper into the tin, smoothing out at the corners.

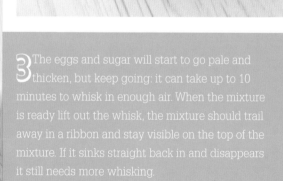

2 Place the eggs and the caster sugar in a large bowl. Air is the only raising agent in a Swiss Roll so get whisking! Don't let the eggs and sugar sit in the bowl together for too long or else the sugar will draw moisture from the eggs and it will take much longer to whisk them up until thick and volumised.

3 The eggs and sugar will start to go pale and thicken, but keep going: it can take up to 10 minutes to whisk in enough air. When the mixture is ready lift out the whisk, the mixture should trail away in a ribbon and stay visible on the top of the mixture. If it sinks straight back in and disappears it still needs more whisking.

4 When the egg and sugar mixture is thick and aerated enough gently sift over the flour.

5 Fold the flour into the mixture using a spatula or metal spoon. Cut through the mixture and turn, lifting the mixture from the bottom of the bowl. Cut through any pockets of flour as you find them. Gently is the way to do it to keep as much air in the mixture as possible.

TIP If the flour is just tipped in the weight of it will make it sink straight to the bottom in a clump and will be difficult to fold in.

6 Once it's fully combined gently transfer the mixture into the prepared tin. Ease the mixture into the corners of the tin by tilting gently, trying to avoid popping any of the bubbles.

7 Bake the cake for 15 minutes. It should be a light golden brown on the top and you should still hear a little 'pfft' when you touch it lightly with a fingertip. We need this moisture for flexibility and rolling. Dry it out completely and it would have to be folded not rolled!

8 The cake should still be warm and it's time to get ready for rolling: take a piece of baking paper slightly larger than the size of the cake and set it on the work surface. Scatter it liberally with caster sugar – this will stop the cake from sticking to the paper.

9 Remove the cake from the tray, still in its baking paper. Gently ease the lining paper away from each edge of the cake, then flip it over so that the top of the cake sits on top of the caster sugar covered sheet. Carefully peel away the paper from the base of the cake. It will still be warm so do be careful.

10 Spread the cake with a good layer of jam. Using a sharp knife, cut a line going halfway through the depth of the cake about 2cm (¾in) from the short end of the cake, all the way along. Fold this small section directly over onto the jam.

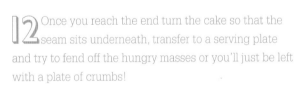

11 Take a firm hold of the baking paper along the short side and begin to roll up the cake. Use your free hand to encourage it to roll. Once it starts simply continue lifting the paper and the cake will roll itself up.

12 Once you reach the end turn the cake so that the seam sits underneath, transfer to a serving plate and try to fend off the hungry masses or you'll just be left with a plate of crumbs!

TIP Because Swiss Rolls are so aerated they should be cut with a sharp serrated knife in a gentle sawing motion to avoid compressing the cake as it is cut.

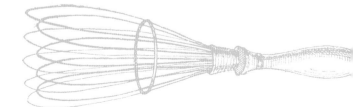

CHOCOLATE, CREAM & STRAWBERRY ROLL

Chocolate, cream and strawberries is a combination made in heaven, though all sorts of fruits could be used instead – just pick your favourite. If you want to add cream to a Swiss Roll you'll need to let the cake cool completely first. There's a knack to not letting the cake dry out completely and causing serious crackage when you roll it – here's how!

MAKES ONE SWISS ROLL
PREP ⏱ 30 MINUTES PLUS COOLING | BAKE ⏱ 15 MINUTES
OVEN 160°C (FAN)/180°C/350°F/GAS MARK 4

INGREDIENTS
Cake
4 eggs, large

100g (3½oz) caster (superfine) sugar

60g (2¼oz) plain (all-purpose) flour

35g (1¼oz) cocoa powder

Filling and rolling
A little caster (superfine) sugar for rolling

300ml (10fl oz) double (heavy) cream

1 tbsp icing (confectioners) sugar

30g (1oz) grated dark chocolate

200g (7oz) strawberries

EQUIPMENT
Electric handmixer

Swiss Roll tin (pan) or shallow-sided roasting tray approx. 33 x 23cm (13 x 9in)

Spreader

1 Follow the same method for the Swiss Roll, but sifting in 60g (2¼oz) plain (all-purpose) flour and 35g cocoa powder.

2 Bake for 15 minutes. Remove it from the oven and set the tin on a cooling rack, don't take out the cake but throw a clean tea towel over the top. This keeps in the moisture whilst the Swiss Roll cools. Allow to cool completely, but don't leave it hours and hours or the moisture will have gone. Keep the Swiss Roll in the tin under the teatowel until you're ready for assembly.

3 Lightly whip the double cream with the icing sugar and hull and quarter the strawberries.

4 Place a sheet of baking paper on the work surface, slightly larger than the Swiss Roll and sprinkle well with caster sugar. Take the Swiss Roll from the tin and loosen the paper from the edges. Flip the cake onto the caster sugar and remove the paper from the base.

5 Spread liberally with the whipped cream, make an incision halfway through the depth of the cake all the way along one short side, about 2cm (¾in) from the left short end of the cake. To the right of the cut add in a line of strawberries and a sprinkle of the chocolate.

6 Take the short end of the baking paper and start to roll up the cake, first folding over the piece to the left of the incision. Roll it over until the line of strawberries and chocolate are tucked inside. Add another row of strawberries and chocolate and continue rolling. Add in more fruit and chocolate as soon as the last line disappears. Once you get to the end of the cake, turn the Swiss Roll over until the seam sits underneath. Transfer to a serving plate and serve.

ANGEL CAKE

. . . .

MAKES ONE 27CM (10¾IN) ROUND CAKE
PREP ⏱ 40 MINUTES PLUS COOLING | BAKE ⏱ 45 MINUTES
OVEN 160°C (FAN)/180°C/350°F/GAS MARK 4

If you think melt in the mouth meringues but in a soft, lighter than air cake form that just about sums up an Angel Cake. Go on, make yourself an Angel today – you'll be pleased you did!

INGREDIENTS
Cake
100g (3½oz) plain (all-purpose) flour
9 egg whites (approx. 310ml/10fl oz)
1½ tsp vanilla extract
1½ tsp vinegar (malt or white wine)
220g (8oz) caster (superfine) sugar

Topping
220g (8oz) jar Raspberry Coulis
220g (8oz) strawberries
100g (3½oz) raspberries
100g (3½oz) redcurrants

EQUIPMENT
Angel Cake/Tube/Ring tin (pan)
   approx. 27cm (10¾in) diameter,
   11.5cm (4½in) depth
Stand / electric whisk
Chopping board
Glass beer bottle

1 Preheat the oven to 160°C (fan)/180°C/350°F/ Gas Mark 4. Starting with the prep, sift the flour three times. Yes, three times, and set to one side.

2 Now for the egg whites: scrupulously clean bowl and whisk please, any trace of grease and they won't whip up for you. Place them in a large bowl along with the vanilla extract and vinegar, and start to whisk. Whisking by machine is easiest!

TIP Vinegar works to stabilise the whisked egg whites by lowering the pH. Cream of Tartar will do the same job, as will lemon, and should be added as the start of whisking. The resulting whisked egg whites will be flexible and stable enough to cope with folding, piping and baking – keeping in all the air bubbles that you've worked hard to incorporate.

3 Once the egg whites start to go white and frothy, with the whisk still running begin to add the sugar just one spoonful at a time, allowing it to be whisked in before adding the next. Slowly does it. Incorporate all the sugar in this way. Whisk it in fully and then continue to whisk until the egg whites will stand in stiff peaks.

4 Sift the flour onto the egg whites and gently fold in using a spatula or metal spoon, cutting through the pockets of flour, lifting and turning until everything is fully incorporated and any major lumps are worked out.

TIP Liquid pasteurised egg whites can be bought in cartons from the refrigerated section in the supermarket which saves you having 9 egg yolks to be used up. Alternatively use up leftover egg yolks to make custard (see Troubleshooting section)

5 Place dollops of the angel mix into the angel cake/tube tin carefully, to avoid knocking out the air. The tin should not be greased, the mixture needs the sides of the cake tin to cling onto and climb up as it rises.

6 Roughly level the mixture with the back of a spoon and bake in the oven for 45 minutes until golden brown and springy when touched lightly with a fingertip.

8 Prepare the fruit. Reserve 8 stems of redcurrants for decoration, then hull and quarter the strawberries, and toss them together with the raspberries and remaining redcurrants.

7 Remove from the oven. Now, to stop it from sinking inwards take a small, squat glass bottle, a beer bottle is ideal. Turn the cake upside down. Trust me, it won't fall out. Place the central tube of the cake tin over the neck of the bottle. Hold it steady and then gently let go. The tin should sit suspended on the top of the bottle. Allow it to cool completely like this.

9 Once the cake has fully cooled remove the tin from the bottle. Using a palette knife loosen the cake from the tin around the sides and gently flip out onto a serving plate. Pour the raspberry coulis over the cake and top with the fruit. Finally lay the reserved redcurrant stems over the top and serve.

TIP Don't use a plastic bottle for inverting the Angel Cake – it'll melt with the heat from the tin!

ORANGE ANGEL

Make a citrus Angel using grated orange zest which perfumes the cake beautifully, or make it lemon if you prefer and finish simply with orange icing for a less dressy affair.

MAKES ONE 27CM (10¾IN) ROUND CAKE
PREP ⏱ 30 MINUTES PLUS COOLING | BAKE ⏱ 45 MINUTES
OVEN 160°C (FAN)/180°C/350°F/GAS MARK 4

TIP
You do need a ring tin/Angel cake pan to bake an Angel in – the structure won't hold up in a large round cake tin. Ring tins are widely available but you could use a Bundt tin instead. If you're investing in a tin a silicone one does the job well and takes up very little cupboard space too.

INGREDIENTS
Cake
100g (3½oz) plain (all-purpose) flour
9 egg whites (approx. 310ml/10fl oz)
Zest of 1 orange
1½ tsp vinegar (malt or white wine)
220g (8oz) caster (superfine) sugar

Topping
150g (5½oz) icing (confectioners) sugar, sifted
Juice from 1 orange
Zest from 1 orange (optional)

EQUIPMENT
Angel Cake/Tube/Ring tin (pan)
   approx. 27cm (10¾in) diameter, 11.5cm (4½in) depth
Stand / electric whisk
Chopping board
Glass beer bottle

1 Following the same method as the regular Angel Cake whip up the egg whites with just the vinegar, omitting the vanilla extract. Once the sugar has been incorporated whisk in the orange zest.

2 Once baked and cooled mix together a glacé icing combining the icing sugar with juice from the orange, adding just a little at a time until you reach a thick, pourable consistency. If you run out of juice, add a little water. Pour over the top of the Orange Angel and finish by grating over a little more orange zest. Serve.

SUMMER FRUIT GENOISE

• •

MAKES ONE 20CM (8IN) CAKE
PREP ⏱ **45 MINUTES PLUS COOLING | BAKE** ⏱ **30–35 MINUTES**
OVEN 160°C (FAN)/180°C/350°F/GAS MARK 4

Genoise sponges are the lightest type of cake you can make – they weigh almost nothing. A little bit tricky to do but follow the steps and you'll be there in no time.

INGREDIENTS
Cake
8 eggs
250g (9oz) caster (superfine) sugar
100g (3½oz) butter, melted and cooled
200g (7oz) plain (all-purpose) flour
100g (3½oz) summer berries –
    blackberries, raspberries,
    blackcurrants etc

Filling and topping
350ml (12fl oz) double (heavy) cream
2 tbsp icing (confectioners) sugar
350g (12oz) summer berries
220g (8oz) blackcurrant preserve

EQUIPMENT
Electric hand mixer
Silicone spatula
3 x 20cm (8in) sandwich tins (layer
    cake pans)

1 Preheat the oven to 160°C (fan)/180°C/350°F/Gas Mark 4. Grease and line the bases of three 20cm (8in) sandwich tins. Check the shelves of the oven, positioning them in the bottom half, making sure you can get all 3 tins in at the same time.

2 Place the eggs and the caster sugar in a large bowl – it does need to be large as the mixture doubles in volume. Using an electric hand mixer begin to whisk the eggs and sugar. Keep whisking: they will turn pale and fluffy but it will take between 5 and 10 minutes. When it's ready the mixture will have doubled in size and as the mixture drops back down from the whisk into the bowl it should fall in a ribbon and the trail will stay visible in the bowl. It takes a while to get to this stage, don't give up – just keep whisking!

TIP **When whisking together the eggs and sugar you can speed things up a bit by placing the bowl on top of a pan of steaming water. It's a bit of a balancing exercise but the heat helps them whisk up faster.**

3 Ensure your butter is properly cooled – if it's added red hot the cake mixture will instantly lose all of its volume and you'll have a bowl of soup instead. Take a large spoonful of the cake mixture and add it to the cooled melted butter. Beat them together vigorously and add this back into the cake mix and fold in. Concentrate on the sides and base of the bowl to check the butter isn't hiding in a pocket anywhere.

4 Now sift half of the flour into the cake mixture and fold in using a spatula, lifting and turning the mixture gently. Make sure you lift the mixture from the very bottom of the bowl. The flour tends to sit here and refuse to budge if you don't keep your eye on it. Once pockets of flour aren't showing up when you fold it sift in the remaining half of the flour and repeat the gentle folding in process.

5 Use two thirds of the cake mixture to fill 2 of the sandwich tins, leaving one third still in the bowl.

TIP
If a pocket of melted butter tricked you and came slooshing out with the cake mixture stir it gently in the tin with the end of a palette knife.

6 Lightly crush the berries for the cake in a small bowl with a fork and fold through the remaining mixture. Fill the final tin and bake straight away in the oven, two on the upper shelf and one just below.

7 After 30 minutes check the cakes – they should be golden on top and springy to the touch, with the sides of the cake shrinking away from the tin. The third cake on the lower shelf may need a further 5 minutes' baking time.

8 Let the cakes cool in the tins for 5 minutes before removing and transferring carefully to a wire rack to cool completely. Once cooled it's time for the assembly.

TIP
**If you missed
a spot when greasing
the edge of the cake will
grip to the side of the tin.
Free it gently with a sharp
knife as soon as it comes
out of the oven.**

9 Softly whip the double cream and icing sugar. Weigh out 150g (5½oz) of the fruit and place in a bowl, then lightly crush with a fork. Fold through the whipped cream to create a ripple effect.

10 Remove the paper from the base of each cake and select a serving plate. Place one of the plain sponge layers on the plate and top with a layer of blackcurrant preserve keeping it just shy of the edge of the cake. Either pipe on a layer of summer berry rippled cream or spread with a spatula.

11 Place the fruited cake layer on top and repeat with a layer of jam and cream. Top with the last plain sponge cake. Cover the top of the cake with the remaining cream in a thin, even layer.

TIP The cream filling means that the cake should be stored in the fridge, so if it isn't possible to assemble it at the last minute, allow the cake 20 minutes to stand at room temperature before serving.

12 Scatter the remaining 200g (7oz) of summer berries around the top of the cake. Serve.

CHOC CHERRY GENOISE

Chocolate and cherries are a fabulous combination, made all the better here by the contrast of lighter than air cake with juicy whole cherries on top.

QUANTITY: MAKES ONE 20 CM (8 IN) CAKE
PREP ⊕ 45 MINUTES | BAKE ⊕ 30–35 MINUTES
OVEN 160°C (FAN)/180°C/350°F/GAS MARK 4

1 Follow the method for the Summer Fruit Genoise but replace the 200g (7oz) plain (all-purpose) flour with a mixture of 120g (¾oz) plain (all-purpose) flour and 80g (3oz) cocoa powder, sifted together. Fold the chopped cherries into a third of the mixture – this is for the middle layer.

2 For the cream filling softly whip the double cream with the icing sugar. Melt 75g (2¾oz) of dark chocolate and set aside to cool a little before stirring through the whipped cream. Set aside 8 whole cherries and roughly chop the remainder.

3 Reserve 100g (3½oz) of the chopped cherries and fold the remaining through the chocolate cream. Assemble the cakes with the cherry studded cake in the middle, applying the cream filling between each.

4 Spread the remaining cream on top of the cake and dust with cocoa. Position the 8 whole cherries around the edge and sprinkle on the reserved roughly chopped cherries. A sprinkle of gold edible glitter is optional but adds a lovely touch of sparkle! Serve.

INGREDIENTS
Cake
8 eggs
250g (9oz) caster (superfine) sugar
100g (3½oz) butter, melted and cooled
120g (4oz) plain (all-purpose) flour
80g (3oz) cocoa powder
100g (3½oz) cherries, pitted and chopped

Filling and topping
350ml (12fl oz) double (heavy) cream
2 tbsp icing (confectioners) sugar
75g (2¾oz) dark chocolate, melted
260g (9oz) cherries
Gold edible glitter for decoration (optional)
Cocoa powder, to dust

EQUIPMENT
Electric hand mixer
Silicone spatula
3 x 20cm (8in) sandwich tins (layer cake pans)

TIP Fresh cherries are ideal but if you don't fancy the hassle of removing the stones tinned or frozen cherries will do the trick.

CARROT CAKE

· ·

MAKES ONE 20CM (8IN) CAKE
PREP ⏱ 40 MINUTES | BAKE ⏱ 1 HOUR 10 MINUTES
OVEN 160°C (FAN)/180°C/350°F/GAS MARK 4

There are certain cakes that benefit hugely from whisking the egg whites separately and then folding in to the finished mixture – carrot cake is one of those so give this version a try!

INGREDIENTS
Cake
200ml (7fl oz) sunflower or
    vegetable oil
65g (2½oz) golden (corn) syrup
2 eggs, large, separated
130g (4½oz) light Muscovado sugar
190g (6½oz) self-raising (-rising)
    flour
1½ tsp cinnamon
½ tsp ground cloves
½ tsp ground ginger
50g (1¾oz) sultanas (golden raisins)
220g (9oz) grated carrot (approx.
    8 small carrots, peeled, topped
    and grated)

Cream cheese frosting
35g (1¼oz) butter
110g (4oz) full fat cream cheese
300g (10½ oz) icing (confectioners)
    sugar, sifted

Carrot Decorations (optional)
25g (1oz) orange sugarpaste
    (rolled fondant)
5g (⅛oz) green sugarpaste (rolled
    fondant)

EQUIPMENT
20cm (8in) round baking tin, at least
    7.5cm (3in) deep
Skewer

1 Preheat the oven to 160°C (fan)/180°C/350°F/Gas Mark 4. Line the base and sides of the cake tin.

TIP

Measure the oil in a jug, add to the bowl and then use the same jug to weigh the golden syrup – the syrup will just slide straight out into the mixing bowl.

2 In a large bowl (make sure it's big enough to fold in the whisked egg whites later on – it's no fun struggling in a small bowl) place the sunflower oil, golden syrup, egg yolks and light Muscovado sugar. Give it a quick mix up and then set it to one side. The mixture will still be coarse and lumpy but don't worry, by the time we come back to it the sugar will have softened and it'll be a breeze to mix together.

3 In a small bowl mix together the self-raising flour, cinnamon, ground cloves, ground ginger and sultanas.

4 In a clean bowl whisk the egg whites until they stand in stiff peaks, and set to one side.

5 Now back to the sugar/oil mixture. Mix it well with a spatula until it's even; it takes a bit of work to get the oil to incorporate but you'll get there.

6 Add the grated carrot to the sugar/oil mixture and mix it up again. Now in goes the flour, spices and sultanas and a final good mix up.

7 Take a third of the whipped egg whites and add to the carrot batter. Beat in briskly with a spatula. This first bit loosens the mixture. Now add the rest of the egg whites and fold in carefully using a spatula to cut through and lift the mixture.

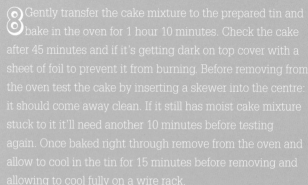

8 Gently transfer the cake mixture to the prepared tin and bake in the oven for 1 hour 10 minutes. Check the cake after 45 minutes and if it's getting dark on top cover with a sheet of foil to prevent it from burning. Before removing from the oven test the cake by inserting a skewer into the centre: it should come away clean. If it still has moist cake mixture stuck to it it'll need another 10 minutes before testing again. Once baked right through remove from the oven and allow to cool in the tin for 15 minutes before removing and allowing to cool fully on a wire rack.

9 To make the cream cheese frosting place the butter in a large bowl and beat it well with a spatula so it's super soft. Add the cream cheese to the bowl and beat the two together until they're fully mixed. Now add in the sifted icing sugar and work it all together until smooth. Spread the cream cheese frosting over the top of the cooled cake with a palette knife.

10 For the carrot decorations divide the 25g (1oz) orange sugarpaste into ten equal pieces. Roll each into a ball in the palm of your hand. To taper one end of the carrot lay the ball in the palm of your hand and roll it underneath a fingertip. Using something pointy (a skewer or the wrong end of a paintbrush) poke a hole in the top of the carrot.

11 To make the leaves divide the green sugarpaste into 10 equal pieces and roll each into a ball. Taper the end of each as with the carrots, set onto a work surface lightly dusted with icing sugar and flatten the ball part with your fingertip. Take a sharp knife and make 3 small cuts into the flattened piece to divide into the leafy part of the carrot.

12 Put a tiny dab of water on the pointy part of the carrot top, and then insert it into the hole in the carrot body, gently squeezing the two parts together. Finally, imprint three lines down the body of the carrot with a knife. Space the decorations evenly around the frosted cake. Serve.

TIP It's important that the butter and cream cheese are the same temperature for them to blend together well. Get them out of the fridge at the same time to soften.

MOIST TOFFEE APPLE CAKE

Come Autumn time and cooking apples are in abundance why not whip up this delicious Moist Toffee Apple cake?

MAKES ONE 20 CM (8 IN) CAKE
PREP ⊕ 30 MINUTES | BAKE ⊕ 1 HOUR 10 MINUTES
OVEN 160°C (FAN)/180°C/350°F/GAS MARK 4

1 Follow the steps for the Carrot Cake replacing the carrot with grated apple and using a combination of wholemeal flour, self-raising flour, baking powder and ground almonds. Apples contain much more water than carrot so the ground almonds are needed to hold the structure.

2 When making the cream cheese frosting use a golden icing sugar if possible for a subtle toffee taste.

3 To make the rosy red apple decorations divide the red sugarpaste into 10 equal pieces, then roll each into a ball in the palm of your hand. Poke a hole in the top of each 'apple' using a skewer.

4 To make the stalks roll small, thin stems in the palm of your hand with your fingertip and insert the end of each into one of the apples. The leaves are small balls of green sugarpaste, flattened with your fingertip and lightly pinched at one end between your thumb and forefinger. Lightly imprint the centre vein of the leaf with a sharp knife and position next to the stalk.

INGREDIENTS

Cake
200ml (7fl oz) sunflower oil
65g (2½oz) clear runny honey
2 eggs, large, separated
130g (4½oz) light muscovado sugar
95g (3¼oz) plain (all-purpose) wholemeal (whole-wheat) flour
95g (3¼oz) self-raising (-rising) flour
100g (3½oz) ground almonds
1½ tsp cinnamon
½ tsp ground cloves
½ tsp baking powder
50g (1¾oz) sultanas (golden raisins)
200g (7oz) grated Bramley apple (approx. 2 medium cooking apples, peeled, cored and grated)

Frosting
35g (1¼oz) butter
110g (4oz) full fat cream cheese
300g (10½oz) icing (confectioners) sugar, sifted

Apple Decorations (optional)
25g (1oz) red sugarpaste (rolled fondant)
5g (⅙oz) green sugarpaste (rolled fondant)

EQUIPMENT
20cm (8in) round baking tin, at least 7.5cm (3in) deep
Skewer

RHUBARB & CUSTARD BOMBE

MAKES ONE BOMBE CAKE
PREP ⏱ 1 HOUR, PLUS CHILLING AT LEAST 4 HOURS, IDEALLY OVERNIGHT | BAKE ⏱ 8–10 MINUTES
OVEN 210°C (FAN)/230°C/450°F/GAS MARK 8

How about a Cake Bombe for a grand show-off dessert? The cake lesson here is a Joconde sponge, a super flexible sheet that can be shaped and moulded all sorts of ways. Here it's filled with my favourite combination of rhubarb and custard, but I'm sure you can come up with all sorts of flavours for the filling!

INGREDIENTS

Vanilla Cream
300ml (10fl oz) double (heavy) cream
1 tsp vanilla bean paste
30g (1oz) icing (confectioners) sugar

Rhubarb Filling
300g (10½oz) rhubarb
50g (1¾oz) caster (superfine) sugar
50ml (2fl oz) water
1 tbsp cornflour (cornstarch)

Custard
100ml (3½fl oz) milk
100ml (3½fl oz) double (heavy) cream
1 tsp vanilla bean paste or the seeds
  scraped from 1 vanilla pod
3 egg yolks, large
45g (1½oz) caster (superfine) sugar
1 tbsp cornflour (cornstarch)

Cake
5 whole eggs, large
185g (6½oz) ground almonds
185g (6½oz) icing (confectioners)
  sugar, sifted
40g (1½oz) butter, melted and cooled
50g (1¾oz) plain (all-purpose) flour,
  sifted
5 egg whites
25g (1oz) caster (superfine) sugar

To Decorate
Mini white chocolate cigarillos
White and pink chocolate curls

EQUIPMENT
Electric stand or hand mixer
Two 30 x 35cm (12 x 14in) baking
  trays 1cm (½in) deep
Baking (parchment) paper
Small, medium and large pans
Cling film (plastic wrap)
1 litre (20fl oz) Pyrex glass bowl
15cm (6in) pastry cutter

1 First make the vanilla cream. Place the double cream, icing sugar and vanilla bean paste into a large bowl and whisk until the mixture forms soft peaks. The consistency should be soft but not runny. Cover the vanilla cream with cling film and store in the fridge until later.

2 Next make the rhubarb filling. In a small bowl or cup mix together the water and cornflour. Cut the trimmed rhubarb stalks into 1.5cm (½in) chunks and place into a medium pan with the caster sugar. Heat the rhubarb gently, stirring occasionally until the sugar dissolves and the rhubarb is softened, only just still holding together. Pour in the water and cornflour and continue to heat until the mixture comes to the boil and thickens. Remove from the heat and transfer to a clean bowl. Cover with cling film, easing it down the sides of the bowl so it is in contact with the rhubarb filling and allow to cool to room temperature.

3 For the custard, measure the milk and cream into a large pan, add the vanilla bean paste and whisk to combine. Place the egg yolks into a large jug and add the caster sugar and cornflour. Whisk it up straight away until even.

4 Now heat the milk/cream in the pan until it's just below boiling point. Take it off the heat and pour it over the egg yolks in the jug a little at a time whilst whisking continuously. This stops the egg from scrambling and ruining your custard. Once all the milk/cream has been added pour the whole lot back into the pan.

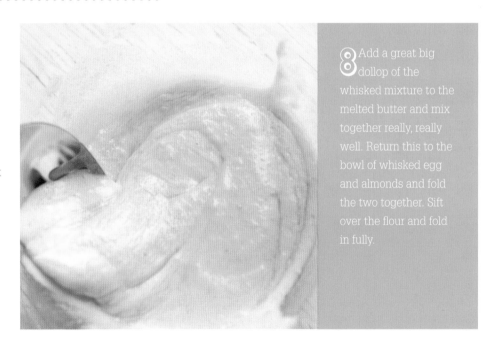

5 Heat it over a gentle heat whilst whisking the whole time. The mixture on the base of the pan will cook faster and thicken so keep whisking – this will stop it getting lumpy. Heat whilst whisking (I think you've got the gist now!) until the custard is nice and thick. Take it off the heat and transfer it to a clean bowl and contact cover with cling film.

6 On to the Joconde sponge. Preheat the oven to 210*C (fan)/230*C/450*F/Gas Mark 8, and line the baking trays with baking paper.

7 Place the whole eggs, ground almonds and icing sugar in a large bowl and whisk until the mixture is extremely thick and volumised – it takes about 8–10 minutes so keep going. Unlike the cake mixture for a Swiss Roll this mix will not quite make it to falling in ribbons, but very nearly!

8 Add a great big dollop of the whisked mixture to the melted butter and mix together really, really well. Return this to the bowl of whisked egg and almonds and fold the two together. Sift over the flour and fold in fully.

9 Now whisk the egg whites until they go foamy. You will need a scrupulously clean bowl and whisks – any speck of grease and the whites won't whisk up properly. Add the caster sugar a spoonful at a time whilst whisking until the whites will stand in firm peaks. So much whisking!

TIP It's easiest to make this sponge with an electric mixer as so much whisking is involved – either a stand mixer or a hand mixer will do the trick.

10 Take a third of the whipped egg whites and quickly beat into the almond mixture until it's evenly combined. Add the rest of the egg whites and this time fold in until the whites have been fully incorporated into the mixture.

11 Divide the mixture between the two baking trays. Instead of trying to spread the cake mixture simply tilt the trays gently to ease the mixture into the corners.

12 Bake each tray one at a time in the oven for 8–10 minutes until lightly golden brown on the top, very gently springy to the touch but not dried out. The crust should not be sticky to the touch. Remove from the oven, keeping them in the trays, and allow to cool fully. Once cooled you can cover them with a clean tea towel if you're not using them right away.

TIP **If your cake lining splits don't panic! If the gap between a split is minimal don't worry it will still hold together. If the gap is wide then patch in a piece from the excess cake you cut away. No-one will ever know.**

13 Line your 1 litre Pyrex glass bowl with cling film. Cut a large sheet of cling film, place your fist into the centre, gather the film around it loosely, place your fist in the bottom of the bowl and unwrap the cling film, allowing a good overlap around the bowl edge. Repeat with a second layer.

14 Lay out a sheet of cling film on the work surface, slightly bigger than the sheet of sponge. Carefully take one sheet of cake out of the tin and flip it face down on the cling film. Release the paper from the edges of the cake, and then begin to peel off the paper, working from each edge into the centre. If you peel from one end it's likely to rip the sheet. Lift the sheet taking care to support it, using the cling film to help you ease it into the bowl. I won't kid you it's a tricky business, slowly and gently is the key. Shape the cake to the bowl, allowing the sheet of cake to pleat where it needs to, easing it with the cling film. Once it's in carefully remove the film you used to help. Take a sharp pair of scissors and trim away the cake level with the top of the bowl. Gently press the pleats towards to the sides of the bowl to flatten a little.

15 Now for the assembly. Place half of the vanilla cream into the base and smooth level with the back of a spoon.

16 Gently stir the cooled rhubarb and add a little at a time on top of the cream, until it is all used up.

17 Beat the custard well with a spoon and add three quarters on top of the rhubarb and smooth it level.

18 Add the remaining custard to the leftover vanilla cream and fold through until it is evenly combined to create a custard cream for covering the bombe later. Set to one side. Remove the second sheet of cake from the tin and loosen the paper at the edges. Cut out two 15cm (6in) circles using a pastry cutter and gently peel away from the backing paper.

19 Carefully lift the first cake disc and place it onto the top of the bombe, sitting on the custard. Apply a thin layer of the custard cream on top of the cake disc. Place the second disc on top of the custard cream. Press gently on the cake circle to level. Reserve the remaining custard cream, storing it in the fridge for later.

20 Gather together the overhanging cling film from around the bowl pulling it over the cake circles tightly all the way around to seal in the cake. Flip the bowl over onto a plate to invert it and place in the fridge to chill for a minimum of 4 hours but ideally overnight.

21 Once chilled, turn the bombe over again and peel away the cling film. Invert onto a serving plate and carefully remove the bowl. Unwrap the clingfilm and discard. Use the remaining custard cream to coat the outside of the entire cake, using a palette knife to smooth. For decoration add a double layer of mini white chocolate cigarillos around the base and top with some white and pink chocolate curls. Chill until you're ready to serve. After all that hard work you deserve a great big slice!

BANOFFEE BOMBE

You can't go wrong with a banoffee filling in this bombe cake!

MAKES ONE BOMBE CAKE
PREP ⏱ **1 HOUR, PLUS CHILLING AT LEAST 4 HOURS**
IDEALLY OVERNIGHT | BAKE ⏱ **8–10 MINUTES**
OVEN 210°C (FAN)/230°C/450°F/GAS MARK 8

1 Make the sheets of Joconde sponge and the vanilla mousse following the directions in the Rhubarb & Custard Bombe.

2 When it comes to the assembly, first add a quarter of the vanilla mousse, followed by a quarter of the caramel. Slice and layer the 2 medium bananas on top of the caramel. Add another quarter of the caramel and finish with a further quarter of the vanilla mousse.

3 Cover the filling with two 15cm (6in) circles of sponge, sandwiching the two together with a thin layer of caramel. Wrap well with cling film and set base down on a plate, chill in the fridge for a minimum of 4 hours, ideally overnight.

4 Whip together the remaining vanilla mousse and the caramel, transfer to a bowl and reserve for later.

5 Once chilled turn out the cake bombe onto a serving plate and remove the cling film. Coat the outside completely with the caramel/vanilla cream using a palette knife to smooth. Add a double layer of mini chocolate cigarillos around the base of the bombe. Dust with cocoa powder and add 3 slices of banana and 2 cigarillos to the top. Serve.

INGREDIENTS

Cake

5 whole eggs, large

185g (6½oz) ground almonds

185g (6½oz) icing (confectioners) sugar, sifted

40g (1½oz) butter, melted and cooled

50g (1¾oz) plain (all-purpose) flour, sifted

5 egg whites

25g (1oz) caster (superfine) sugar

Vanilla Mousse

100ml (3½fl oz) double (heavy) cream

1 tsp vanilla bean paste or the seeds scraped from 1 vanilla pod

30g (1oz) caster (superfine) sugar

1½ tsp vege-gel

200ml (7fl oz) double (heavy) cream, softly whipped

Banoffee

2 medium bananas, sliced

1 x 297g (10½oz) can of caramel

To Decorate

Mini white and dark chocolate cigarillos

Cocoa powder to dust

3 slices of banana

EQUIPMENT

Electric stand or hand mixer

Two 30 x 35cm (12 x 14in) baking trays 1cm (½in) deep

Small, medium and large pans

Cling film (plastic wrap)

1 litre (20fl oz) Pyrex glass bowl,

15cm (6in) pastry cutter

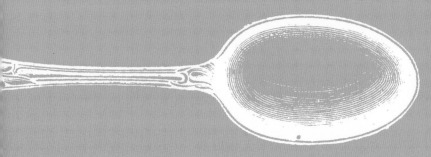

MELTING METHOD

Melting method cakes are probably the quickest to make and take minimum effort: butter and sugars are melted together gently in a pan whilst the dry ingredients are mixed together separately. The finished cake mixture is more batter-like than other cakes and can be poured straight from the bowl into the tin for baking. And the results are deliciously moist!

GOLDEN SYRUP LOAF CAKE

· ·

MAKES ONE 900G (2LB) LOAF CAKE
PREP ⏱ 15 MINUTES | BAKE ⏱ 40 MINUTES
OVEN 160°C (FAN)/180°C /350°F/GAS MARK 4

A gorgeous soft squishy golden syrup cake and as a bonus it's egg-free – perfect for those with allergies or for when you want to bake but are all out of eggs. It might be an impossible task but if you can save the eating till a day after baking the crust goes soft and squidgy too.

INGREDIENTS
Cake
75g (2¾oz) butter
50g (1¾oz) caster (superfine) sugar
150g (5½oz) golden (corn) syrup
100ml (3½fl oz) boiling water
200g (7oz) plain (all-purpose) flour
½ tsp baking powder
½ tsp bicarbonate of soda

EQUIPMENT
900g (2lb) loaf tin (pan),
   18.5 x 11.5cm (7 x 4½in)
Medium pan

TIP Carefully weighing the butter, sugar, syrup and water directly into the pan will save on the washing up! 100ml (3½fl oz) of water will weigh 100g (3½oz).

1 Preheat the oven to 160°C (fan)/180°C/350°F/Gas Mark 4. Line the tin with baking paper. Place the flour, bicarbonate of soda and baking powder in a large bowl. Use a whisk to lightly mix them together – distributing the raising agents evenly.

2 Weigh out the butter, sugar, syrup and boiling water and place them all in a medium sized pan. Heat over a gentle heat stirring occasionally until the butter and sugar have both melted and the mixture is evenly combined.

3 Remove from the heat and pour over the flour and raising agents.

4 Whisk together, working out the lumps until it's all nice and even.

5 Pour into the prepared tin, pop it in the oven and set the timer!

6 Once baked allow it to cool in the tin a little before carefully lifting out using the lining paper and set onto a wire rack to cool completely. Serve.

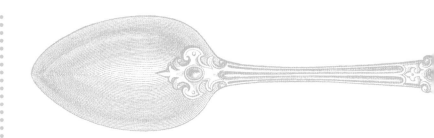

GINGER TREACLE CAKE

For those who like things a little darker and spicier give this ginger treacle cake a go.

MAKES ONE 900G (2LB) LOAF CAKE
PREP ⏱ 15 MINUTES PLUS COOLING | BAKE ⏱ 40 MINUTES
OVEN 160°C (FAN)/180°C/350°F/GAS MARK 4

INGREDIENTS

75g (2¾oz) butter
50g (1¾oz) light Muscovado sugar
75g (2¾oz) golden (corn) syrup
75g (2¾oz) black treacle (blackstrap molasses)
100ml (3½fl oz) boiling water
200g (7oz) plain (all-purpose) flour
½ tsp baking powder
½ tsp bicarbonate of soda
2 tsp ground ginger

EQUIPMENT

900g (2lb) loaf tin (pan), 18.5 x 11.5cm (7 x 4½in)
Medium pan

❚ Follow the same method for the Golden Syrup Cake, but replace half the quantity of syrup with treacle and add 1 tsp of ground ginger to the flour, baking powder and bicarbonate of soda.

TIP
Go to town with the ginger if you like it fiery, adding in 3 tsp instead of 2.

CHOCOLATE ORANGE BROWNIE CAKE

• •

MAKES ONE 20CM (8IN) CAKE
PREP ⏱ 15 MINUTES PLUS COOLING | BAKE ⏱ 35 MINUTES
OVEN 180°C (FAN)/200°C/400°F/GAS MARK 6

Bursting with orange flavour – using a whole orange, skin and all in a recipe may seem a little strange but trust me it works brilliantly!

INGREDIENTS
200g (7oz) dark (semisweet) chocolate, around 49% cocoa solids
140g (5oz) butter
225g (8oz) light Muscovado sugar
85g (3oz) plain (all-purpose) flour
3 eggs, large
1 whole orange

EQUIPMENT
20cm (8in) round cake tin (cake pan), at least 5cm (2in) deep
Baking (parchment) paper
Electric food processor or stick blender

1 Preheat the oven to 180°C (fan)/200°C/400°F/ Gas Mark 6. Grease and line the sides and base of the cake tin.

TIP **Using a 49% cocoa solids chocolate is best for this recipe unless you like a darker tasting chocolate. You can use a 70%+ cocoa solids chocolate but make sure it's a cooks version otherwise it might split when melted in the pan.**

2 Place the chocolate and butter in a medium pan and heat over a gentle heat, stirring frequently until completely melted. Remove from the heat.

3 In a separate bowl stir together the flour and sugar. Add this to the chocolate / butter pan and mix well.

TIP
Stirring the
flour and sugar together
before adding them to the
chocolate / butter mixture
stops you getting lumps of flour
in the mixture that can be a
monkey to get out!

4 Add the eggs to the mixture in the pan and beat well until they're fully combined.

5 Now for the orange. Remove the brown stalky bit and chop it into quarters, then each quarter into half so you have 8 chunks of orange. Blitz the pieces in a food processor or with a handheld stick blender until they are the consistency of a chunky marmalade.

6 Add the blitzed orange to the mixture in the pan and stir well. Pour into the tin and bake in the preheated oven for 35 minutes.

7 Once baked, allow time to cool the cake fully in the tin before removing and serving.

BANANA & CARDAMOM CHOCOLATE BROWNIE CAKE

Chocolate is so versatile that many flavours can be paired with it, transforming the flavour of this brownie cake – blackberries, raspberries, peaches… the list goes on! Here I've gone with banana and cardamom; it's always handy to have a recipe to use up the ripening bananas in the fruit bowl that everyone promised they'd eat three days ago!

MAKES ONE 20 CM (8 IN) CAKE
PREP 🕐 **15 MINUTES PLUS COOLING | BAKE** 🕐 **35 MINUTES**
OVEN 160°C (FAN)/180°C/350°F/GAS MARK 4

INGREDIENTS

200g (7oz) dark (semisweet) chocolate, around 49% cocoa solids
140g (5oz) butter
seeds from 6 cardamom pods, crushed
225g (8oz) soft light brown sugar
85g (3oz) plain flour
3 eggs, large
3 ripe bananas, peeled weight approx. 300g (10½oz), mashed

EQUIPMENT

20cm (8in) round cake tin (cake pan), at least 5cm (2in) deep
Baking (parchment) paper
Electric food processor or stick blender
Pestle and mortar

Follow the same method as Chocolate Orange Brownie Cake, but add the crushed cardamom seeds to the pan with the chocolate and butter, and add the mashed banana in place of the orange.

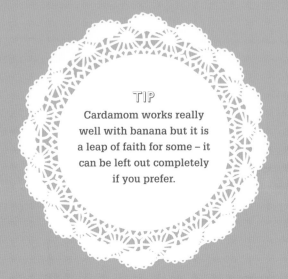

TIP
Cardamom works really well with banana but it is a leap of faith for some – it can be left out completely if you prefer.

JEWELLED FRUIT LOAF

MAKES ONE 900G (2LB) LOAF CAKE
PREP 🕐 20 MINUTES PLUS OVERNIGHT SOAKING
BAKE 🕐 1 HOUR 10 MINUTES
OVEN 160°C (FAN)/180°C/350°F/GAS MARK 4

Packed with fruit and nuts this cake is a real gem when you slice it up. Soaking the fruit overnight plumps it up so it's sweet and juicy – but don't worry if you forget, there's a magic trick for that!

INGREDIENTS

50g (1¾oz) dried apricots
100g (3½oz) sultanas (golden raisins)
70g (2½oz) dried cranberries
35g (1¼oz) dried cherries
300ml (10fl oz) pomegranate juice
45g (1½oz) glacé (candied) cherries, halved
45g (1½oz) whole almonds, roughly chopped
75g (2¾oz) butter
125g (4½oz) caster (superfine) sugar
1 large egg
225g (8oz) self-raising (-rising) flour
15g (½oz) nibbed sugar

EQUIPMENT

900g (2lb) loaf tin (pan),
    18.5 x 11.5cm (7 x 4½in)
Medium pan

1 Chop the apricots into pieces roughly the same size as the sultanas and mix together with the sultanas, dried cherries and cranberries in a bowl. Pour over the pomegranate juice, stir and cover. Leave to soak overnight.

2 By the next day the fruit will be lovely and plump and have absorbed the majority of the juice. Not only does the soaking of the fruit make it flavoursome and tender but it also stops the fruit from absorbing moisture from the cake batter, making the finished cake dry.

TIP Forgot to soak your fruit or want to bake straight away? No probs! Place the fruit and juice in a small pan and heat very, very gently. Keep your eye on it: you don't want it to boil. The fruit will start to absorb the juice and plump up. Keep heating until the juice surrounding the fruit is reduced by two thirds. Remove from the heat and you're ready to go. Just be careful when you add the egg – be sure to allow the mixture to cool sufficiently otherwise you'll have cake mixture containing scrambled egg!

3 Preheat the oven to 160°C (fan)/180°C/350°F/Gas Mark 4. Line a loaf tin with baking paper or a paper liner. Add to the fruit mixture the halved cherries and roughly chopped almonds and give it a good stir. (These are added after the overnight soaking because they wouldn't slurp up any of the juice anyway!)

4 Place the butter and sugar in a medium sized pan and heat gently until the butter has melted and the sugar is starting to dissolve.

5 Remove from the heat and add the fruits and juice. Mix it well, this will cool the mixture enough so that the egg can be added safely without cooking in the heat of the pan. Add the egg and stir until evenly worked in.

TIP Nibbed sugar is much easier to lay your hands on these days but if you can't find any take a small handful of sugar cubes and crush roughly in a plastic sandwich bag with a rolling pin and use to scatter over the top of the loaf cake before baking.

6 Add the flour and mix well again. Place the mixture into the prepared tin, roughly level with the back of a spoon and scatter the nibbed sugar over the top.

7 Bake in the oven for 1 hour and 10 minutes, or until a skewer when inserted comes away clean. Cover the top of the cake with a sheet of foil after 40 minutes to prevent it from browning too much. Transfer to a wire rack and allow to cool completely. Serve.

TEABREAD

A classic loaf cake to have in your repertoire, the wholemeal flour in this recipe gives the loaf a delicious nutty taste too. Great if you're a tea fiend like me!

MAKES ONE 900G (2LB) LOAF CAKE
PREP ⏲ 20 MINUTES PLUS OVERNIGHT SOAKING
BAKE ⏲ 1 HOUR 10 MINUTES
OVEN 160°C (FAN)/180°C/350°F/GAS MARK 4

TIP
Use your favourite tea for this loaf cake – a strong, flavoursome tea like Twinings Everyday or Yorkshire Tea works really well but you could try Earl Grey, Assam or a fruity Lady Grey.

INGREDIENTS

140g (5oz) sultanas (golden raisins)

120g (4oz) raisins

40g (1½oz) currants

300ml (10fl oz) strong tea

75g (2¾oz) butter

125g (4½oz) soft light brown sugar

1 large egg

225g (8 oz) plain (all-purpose) wholemeal (whole-wheat) flour

2 tsp baking powder

15g (½oz) demerara sugar

Soak all the fruit overnight in the strong tea. Then follow the method for the Jewelled Fruit Cake. You'll need 2 tsp of baking powder to go along with the wholemeal flour though – don't forget! Scatter with demerara sugar before baking for 1 hour and 10 minutes, and make sure you cover the top with a sheet of foil after 40 minutes to prevent it from browning too much.

SUPPLIERS

THE PINK WHISK SHOP
www.thepinkwhiskshop.com
Tel: 0844 880 5852
For tins and baking equipment to get you started – and lots more besides! All products are chosen by me especially for you.

Kenwood Ltd
New Lane
Havant
Hampshire
PO9 2NH
www.kenwoodworld.com/uk
Tel: 02392 476 000
For kitchen electricals

Wright's Flour
GR Wright & Sons Ltd
Ponders End Mills
Enfield
Middlesex
EN3 4TG
Tel: 0800 064 0100
www.wrightsflour.co.uk
For British grown and milled flours

Baking Mad
The Baking Mad Kitchen
Sugar Way
Peterborough
PE2 9AY

Tel: 0800 880 5944
www.bakingmad.com
For Silver Spoon, Billington's, Nielsen-Massey extracts and flavoured chocolate buttons!

BakeryBits
BakeryBits Ltd
1 Orchard Units
Duchy Road
Honiton
Devon, EX14 1YD
UK
Tel: 01404 565656
www.bakerybits.co.uk
For nibbed sugar and other baking equipment

US
Michaels
Michaels Stores, Inc.
8000 Bent Branch Dr.
Irving
TX 75063
Tel: (1-800-642-4235)
www.michaels.com

A C Moore Arts & Crafts
Stores across the US
Tel: 1-888-226-667
www.acmoore.com

Williams-Sonoma
Locations across the US
Tel: 877-812-6235
www.williams-sonoma.com
Bakeware, kitchenware and kitchen electricals

AUSTRALIA
Kitchen Witch
500 Hay Street
Subiaco WA 6008
Tel: 08 9380 4788
www.homeinwa.com.au

Myer
Stores across Australia
PO Box 869J
Melbourne VIC 3001
Phone: 1800 811 611
www.myer.com.au
For bakeware and other baking essentials

Target
Stores across Australia
Customer Relations
Reply Paid 41
Nth Geelong Vic 3215.
Tel: 1800 814 788
www.target.com.au

ABOUT THE AUTHOR

Ruth Clemens is Mum of 3 naughty boys and wife to 1! A passionate self-taught baker and cake decorator, Ruth was a contestant and finalist on the very first series of the BBC's *The Great British Bake Off*. Her first book, *The Busy Girls' Guide to Cake Decorating* was published in April 2012.

Ruth writes the very popular baking blog The Pink Whisk which was featured in *The Independent*'s Top 50 Best Food Websites.

To keep up to date with Ruth's most recent adventures you can join the gang at facebook.com/ThePinkWhisk or on Twitter @thepinkwhisk. And for lots more baking inspiration and recipes visit www.thepinkwhisk.co.uk

ACKNOWLEDGEMENTS

My thanks go to a whole bunch of fab people that have helped me along the way with this book. To my boys for eating cake non-stop for a good long while until they reached the point of saying 'please, no more cake' (Yes that really can happen!).

To David & Charles for agreeing to work with me on a recipe book packed full of step-by-step photos in the first place, and to the team that kept me on the straight and narrow: Judith, Verity, Pru, Sarah, Ame, Ali and Katy.

Lorna and Jack for the gorgeous photos, making every cake come alive on the page, just the way I imagined it.

To the super dooper Louise Brimelow for her help in the kitchen on shoots – can you get me/weigh me/wash that up/mix me – I hope I wasn't too much of a task master!

To Kenwood for the Pink K-Mix and Hand mixer – really making me The Pink Whisk.

Big thanks go to Wright's for the endless supply of flour and to Silver Spoon, Billington's and Nielsen-Massey for lots more ingredients that made these cakes possible.

Still there? Good, I'm not quite finished yet!

To Lucy, Ange & Kate, friends overseas who gave me the tip off where to shop!

And finally to 'The Pink Whiskers', readers of the blog, who have made it possible for me to write a book, for their support and words of encouragement when I most need it – You're a fab bunch of people and I'm proud to say you're my gang!

INDEX

A DAVID & CHARLES BOOK
© F&W Media International, LTD 2013

David & Charles is an imprint of F&W Media International, LTD
Brunel House, Forde Close, Newton Abbot, TQ12 4PU, UK

F&W Media International, Ltd is a subsidiary of F+W Media, Inc
10151 Carver Road, Suite #200, Blue Ash, OH 45242, USA

ISBN-13: 978-1-4463-0279-8 Hardback
ISBN-10: 1-4463-0279-2 Hardback

ISBN-13: 978-1-4463-0311-5 Paperback
ISBN-10: 1-4463-0311-X Paperback

10 9 8 7 6 5 4 3 2 1

Publisher Alison Myer
Junior Acquisitions Editor Verity Graves-Morris
Project Editor Katy Denny
Creative Manager Prudence Rogers
Production Manager Bev Richardson
Photographer Lorna Yabsley / Jack Kirby

Printed in China by RR Donnelley for:
F&W Media International LTD,
Brunel House, Forde Close, Newton Abbot, TQ12 4PU, UK

F+W Media publishes high quality books on a wide range of subjects.
For more great book ideas visit: **www.rucraft.co.uk**